my itty-bitty bio

George H. W. Bush

Published in the United States of America by Cherry Lake Publishing
Ann Arbor, Michigan
www.cherrylakepublishing.com

Reading Adviser: Marla Conn, MS, Ed, Literacy specialist, Read-Ability, Inc.
Book Designer: Jennifer Wahl
Illustrator: Jeff Bane

Photo Credits: ©National Archives Catalog/National Archives ID: 186376, 5; ©U.S. Navy/Joint Base San Antonio, 7; ©National Archives Catalog/National Archives ID: 186384, 9; © George Bush Presidential Library and Museum/HS377, 11; ©George Bush Presidential Library and Museum/H090, 13; © National Archives Catalog/National Archives ID: 198518, 15, 22; ©Library of Congress/Wikimedia/Public Domain, 17, 23; ©National Archives Catalog/National Archives ID: 186464, 19; ©mark reinstein/Shutterstock, 21; Jeff Bane, cover, 1, 6, 10, 14

The appearance of U.S. Department of Defense (DoD) visual information does not imply or constitute DoD endorsement.

Library of Congress Cataloging-in-Publication Data

Names: Sarantou, Katlin, author. | Bane, Jeff, 1957- illustrator.
Title: George H.W. Bush / by Katlin Sarantou ; illustrated by Jeff Bane.
Description: Ann Arbor, [MI] : Cherry Lake Publishing, [2019] | Series: My itty-bitty bio | Includes bibliographical references and index. | Audience: Grades K-3.
Identifiers: LCCN 2019004199| ISBN 9781534147065 (hardcover) | ISBN 9781534148499 (pdf) | ISBN 9781534149922 (pbk.) | ISBN 9781534151352 (hosted ebook)
Subjects: LCSH: Bush, George, 1924-2018--Juvenile literature. | Presidents--United States--Juvenile literature.
Classification: LCC E882 .S27 2019 | DDC 973.928092 [B] --dc23
LC record available at https://lccn.loc.gov/2019004199

Printed in the United States of America
Corporate Graphics

table of contents

About the author: Katlin Sarantou grew up in the cornfields of Ohio. She enjoys reading and dreaming of faraway places.

About the illustrator: Jeff Bane and his two business partners own a studio along the American River in Folsom, California, home of the 1849 Gold Rush. When Jeff's not sketching or illustrating for clients, he's either swimming or kayaking in the river to relax.

my story

I was born in Massachusetts in 1924.

I was named after my grandfather.

What's the story behind your name?

I joined the U.S. Navy when I was 18. I was the youngest **pilot**. I flew 58 **combat missions** during World War II.

I went to Yale University.

I fell in love with Barbara Pierce. We married. We had six children.

My family moved to Texas in 1948.

I started my own oil company.

What's a company you would like to start?

I entered **politics**. I held many important roles.

I served two terms in **Congress**.

What is something you are interested in?

I served as vice president under President Ronald Reagan.

I became president after him.

As president, I passed laws.
I helped people with **disabilities**.
I helped schools.

I only served one term. I lost the next election.

The country had too many problems. I couldn't solve them all.

But I helped shape America. I left behind a political **legacy**.

My son followed in my footsteps. George W. Bush became the 43rd president.

I died on November 30, 2018.
I spent my life serving my country.

What would you like to ask me?

timeline

1981

1920

Born
1924

1989

2020

Died
2018

glossary & index

glossary

combat missions (KAHM-bat MISH-uhnz) military activities that involve capturing or defending something

Congress (KAHNG-gris) the lawmaking part of the U.S. government, made up of the House of Representatives and the Senate

disabilities (dis-uh-BIL-ih-teez) physical or mental conditions that limit a person's movements or senses

legacy (LEG-uh-see) the impact of someone's life

pilot (PYE-luht) a person who flies aircraft

politics (PAH-lih-tiks) having to do with government and laws

index